Dear Parents and Educators,

Welcome to Penguin Young Readers! As parents and educators, you know that each child develops at his or her own pace—in terms of speech, critical thinking, and, of course, reading. Penguin Young Readers recognizes this fact. As a result, each Penguin Young Readers book is assigned a traditional easy-to-read level (1–4) as well as a Guided Reading Level (A–P). Both of these systems will help you choose the right book for your child. Please refer to the back of each book for specific leveling information. Penguin Young Readers features esteemed authors and illustrators, stories about favorite characters, fascinating nonfiction, and more!

## Where the Buffalo Roam: Bison in America

**LEVEL 4**

GUIDED READING LEVEL **P**

This book is perfect for a **Fluent Reader** who:
• can read the text quickly with minimal effort;
• has good comprehension skills;
• can self-correct (can recognize when something doesn't sound right); and
• can read aloud smoothly and with expression.

Here are some **activities** you can do during and after reading this book:
• Using a Glossary: A glossary, like a dictionary, tells you what words mean. Look at the words and their definitions in the glossary at the back of this book. Then write an original sentence for each word.
• Comprehension: After reading this book, answer the following questions:
  • Where do bison live?
  • When do bison form larger herds?
  • What predators can take down a bison?
  • What is one reason that bison stampede?
  • What does *wallowing* mean?
  • What month are most bison born?
  • How did American Indians honor bison?

Remember, sharing the love of reading with a child is the best gift you can give!

—Sarah Fabiny, Editorial Director
   Penguin Young Readers program

*Penguin Young Readers are leveled by independent reviewers applying the standards developed by Irene Fountas and Gay Su Pinnell in *Matching Books to Readers: Using Leveled Books in Guided Reading*, Heinemann, 1999.

PENGUIN YOUNG READERS
An Imprint of Penguin Random House LLC

🌼 Smithsonian

This trademark is owned by the Smithsonian Institution and is registered
in the U.S. Patent and Trademark Office.

Smithsonian Enterprises:
Christopher Liedel, President
Carol LeBlanc, Senior Vice President, Education and Consumer Products
Brigid Ferraro, Vice President, Education and Consumer Products
Ellen Nanney, Licensing Manager
Kealy Gordon, Product Development Manager

Smithsonian's National Zoological Park:
Gilbert Myers, Assistant Curator, Cheetah Conservation Station and American Bison
Jen Zoon, Communications Specialist, Office of Communications

Photo credits: American Bison Coalition: page 30 (top). Library of Congress: pages 25, 26, 27.
National Park Service: pages 11, 16: Neal Herbert; page 30 (bottom): Jacob W. Frank; page 31:
Jim Peaco. Smithsonian Institution Archives: page 28. Thinkstock: cover: dmbaker/iStock;
pages 3, 4, 13 (top): Betty4240/iStock; page 7: Ivan Tykhyi/Hemera; page 8: Matt Gush/iStock;
page 9 (top): Jason Cheever/iStock; page 9 (bottom): twildlife/iStock; page 10: jropelato1/iStock;
page 12: bjlanes/iStock; page 13 (bottom, left): robertcicchetti/iStock; page 13 (bottom, right):
Jupiterimages/liquidlibrary; page 14: GaryLantz/iStock; page 15: Byrdyak/iStock; page 17:
ablokhin/iStock; page 19: jacek76/iStock; page 20: htrnr/iStock; page 21: ChrisBoswell/iStock;
page 22: belfasteileen/iStock; page 23 (top): awalby/iStock; page 23 (bottom): mirceax/iStock;
page 24: JohanWElzenga/iStock; page 29: Exploder1/iStock; page 32: befehr/iStock.

*Library of Congress Cataloging-in-Publication Data is available.*

ISBN 9780515158991 (pbk)     10 9 8 7 6 5 4 3 2 1
ISBN 9780515159004 (hc)      10 9 8 7 6 5 4 3 2 1

## Smithsonian

# Where the Buffalo Roam

## Bison in America

by Kate Waters

Penguin Young Readers
An Imprint of Penguin Random House

4

# Contents

# Introduction

Do you know the old cowboy song "Home on the **Range**"? The title of this book comes from that song.

Many people besides cowboys call this animal a buffalo. But its real name is American bison. In this book, we will use bison, as scientists do.

# Where the Bison Roam

A very old American Indian rock painting of a bison

Bison live in North America. They have been here for more than 250,000 years. Long ago, they roamed the whole **continent** from Canada to Mexico.

Bison can live almost anywhere as long as there is food and water. It doesn't matter to them if the weather is cold or hot.

Bison gather in small **herds** of females and their young for part of the year. When it is **mating** season, they form larger herds.

As bison herds move, they chew and grind grasses, weeds, and other plants. They swallow this food. Then they bring it up and chew and grind it again. This helps them get the most **nutrition** from the plants.

Bison don't have front teeth to cut off stems or leaves. They wrap their strong tongues around a plant and pull!

# Large, Strong, and Fast

Bison are the largest land animals **native** to North America.

A male can be 6 feet tall and 12 feet long. It can weigh up to 2,000 pounds.

male

The female is smaller at 5 feet tall. It can weigh up to 1,200 pounds.

female

calf

Only two kinds of wild **predators** can take down a bison. One is a grizzly bear. The other is a pack of wolves.

Wolves look for a bison that is young or old or weak. They separate it from the herd and attack.

Bison **stampede** when they sense danger. They can run fast for such large animals.

A herd's top speed can be 35 miles an hour. That is faster than a horse **gallops**.

If bison are face-to-face with a
predator, they use their strong horns
to attack.

Bison horns are sharp. They can rip
and stab another animal.

A bison has a hump on the back of its neck. Inside is solid muscle and bone.

The hump helps the bison lift its huge head to sniff for danger.

In winter, a bison uses its head as a snowplow to uncover food.

Bison use their short tails as flyswatters when flies and ticks bite.

Bison also **signal** the herd with their tails.

Tail down? The bison is calm.

Tail up? The bison is excited.

When a bison is really itchy, it rolls in the dirt or mud.

It can't roll over because of its hump. So, it rolls and scratches on one side. Then on the other.

This is called **wallowing**.

# From Calf to Adult

Summer is **breeding** season for bison. They gather in large groups.

Males fight each other. The winner will get to mate with the most females.

First the two males stare at each other. Then they raise and lower their big heads. They paw the ground with their hoofs and let out loud **bellows**.

At this point, one male bison can turn away. If not, both bison lower their heads. Charge!

Most bison young are born in May. Their eyes are open and they usually stand up right away.

When a bison calf runs, it seems to bounce along the ground.

The calf will stay close to its mother for one year. Then another calf will be born.

# Bison and People

Before white people came to America, bison and American Indians roamed the land together. Bison were the center of a whole way of life.

bison horns

bison skin

American Indians worked together on bison hunts.

Every part of the animal was eaten or used. Tipis, clothes, weapons, soap, tools, and toys were made from bison parts.

American Indians honored this very important animal with stories, songs, dances, and prayers.

Then white settlers moved west.

Some killed bison for food or to use their **hides**. Others killed them for sport.

The United States government had many, many bison killed. This took away everything that was important to many American Indians.

Settlers wanted tribal lands for themselves.

In 100 years, the number of bison went from millions to fewer than 1,000.

# Bringing Back Bison

In 1891, the Smithsonian decided to help protect bison. They brought bison to the National Mall in Washington, DC. The animals then moved to a good home at the Smithsonian's National Zoo.

Bison graze in front of the Smithsonian in Washington, DC.

**Conservationists** gathered other bison to shelter them. Slowly, bison numbers increased.

Today, bison herds continue to grow. Bison are protected in national and state parks, in zoos, and on private ranches.

Some American Indian Nation tribes manage bison herds on their land.

The bison is an important symbol of US history.

On May 9, 2016, President Barack Obama signed a bill. It made the bison the first national mammal of the United States.

When you go where bison roam, you can hear them. Bison squeak when they're scared. They snort when they're playful. And they may bellow to let you know they're there!

# Glossary

**bellows:** deep, loud sounds made by animals

**breeding:** mating animals to produce young animals

**conservationists:** people who protect animals and plants from being harmed or wiped out entirely

**continent:** one of the seven great land masses on earth

**gallops:** runs fast

**herds:** large numbers of animals that stay together

**hides:** the skins of animals

**mating:** joining together to produce babies

**native:** from a specific place

**nutrition:** food that living creatures need to survive

**predators:** animals that live by hunting other animals for food

**range:** an area of open land

**signal:** to do something that shows feeling or meaning

**stampede:** a sudden rush of animals in one direction, usually out of fear

**wallowing:** rolling around in dirt or mud